Customer Service for Small Bu

Loyal Raving Fans

27 Ways To Excite And Delight Your Customers

Sarah Bauling

www.ricksmithbooks.com

Sarah Bauling

Copyright © 2015 Sarah Bauling

The aforementioned persons have asserted their rights under the Copyright, Designs & Patent Act 1988 to be identified as the Authors of this work.

This book is sold subject to the conditions that it shall not, by way of trade or otherwise, be lent, resold, hired out, or otherwise circulated without the Publisher's prior consent in any form of binding or cover other than that in which it is published and without a similar condition, including this condition, being imposed on the subsequent purchaser.

Published by Rick Smith Books & Publishing

www.ricksmithbooks.com

Table of Contents

1 Convenience 13
2 Creating A Comfortable Buying Environment 16
3 What Options Do You Offer? 19
4 Keep Your Client In The Loop 22
5 Ask 26
6 Would You Want To Do Business With You? 30
7 Be Prepared To Go The Extra Mile 32
8 Listen To Customer Complaints 35
9 Make Sure Your Middle Man Keeps His Word 38
10 Make It Memorable 41
11 The Unexpected Is What Delights Customers 44
12 Serve Fully 47
13 Treat Every Client As If They Are Your Top Client 50
14 P's And Q's 54
15 Sometimes The Client DOESN'T Want To Talk To You .. 57
16 Get Feedback 60
17 Make Exceptions 65
18 Be Helpful 68
19 You Never Know WHO Your Customer REALLY Is! 71
20 Treat People As You Would Like To Be Treated! 74
21 What Does Your Client Actually Need? 77

22 Motivation 79
23 Maximize 83
24 Who Is Accountable? 86
25 I Can't Do It! 89
26 Smile 92
27 Say What You Are Going To Do And Do It! 95

About the Author

Sarah Bauling is a sought-after Speaker and Trainer in the Customer Service arena. With twenty years of sales and marketing experience in the hospitality industry, Sarah understands the importance of Exciting and Delighting your Customers, and now she shares her professional Weapons of Influence for the first time in print.

Sarah has an Associate degree in Speech and Drama from Trinity College, London, and is an active member of Toastmasters International in South Africa, her homeland.

Sarah speaks and trains widely, with a diverse client list throughout the medical, hospitality, banking, leisure & tourism, and travel industries. You can connect with Sarah, or find out more about her, below:

E-Mail: sarah@sarahspeaks.co.za
Website: www.sarahspeaks.co.za
Twitter: @sarahbauling
Facebook: www.facebook.com/sarahbaulingspeaks
YouTube: sarah bauling

Sarah Bauling

Introduction

The opportunity to write a book on customer service is a project that truly excites me!

Apart from the fact that it gives me the opportunity to share some of my views on my favourite subject, it also gives me the platform to honour those who have inspired me to be the best customer service speaker, trainer, and author I can be.

I was born into an entrepreneurial family. My mom and dad started the first hot-air ballooning company in South Africa, and before I could walk and talk, my older brother Sam and I constantly heard how they spoke to clients, how they spoke about clients, and how they valued each and every person who came into their business. We realised that customers made a business, and if you didn't have customers, you didn't have a business. We also learnt that if we didn't have a business, there would simply be no food on the table. Their attitude towards potential guests, guests who were experiencing it here and now, right through to past customers was awe-inspiring, and to be honest, Sam and I had the two most amazing influencers in our lives.

I grew up, and when it was time to look for a job, I had developed such a love for what my parents did and for making our clients' dreams come true that it was natural I would join the family business.

Shortly after leaving school, I decided to purchase a property and rent it out – I knew nothing about owning a property but applied the same customer service skills I had been exposed to for eighteen years in the family business. My tenants – who in this instance were my clients - were delighted that I listened to them, that I fixed leaking toilets, burst geysers, and made sure the gardeners kept the grounds looking good. They knew that no matter what the problem was, I would sort it out for them as quickly and efficiently as possible. I eventually purchased five homes for rent, and I pride myself in the fact that I have had very few tenants; they stick around because I make their living experience pleasant.

At the age of twenty-one, my love of dancing led me to train as a Ballroom and Latin teacher. I joined Fred Astaire Dance Schools and loved it. Eventually, after being swept off my feet on the dance floor by the man of my dreams, we decided to open our own dance school specialising in social couples.

Within three years, we grew our 'garage dance studio' to thirty-six couples, teaching three times a week, and three group classes a night. By now, we decided to sell the studio and start a family. We sold it to a lady teacher who had the same qualifications, but sadly within three months the studio closed. This surprised me, and when I bumped into students, they said she was a good teacher but lacked the care that Leonard and I had given them, which to us had been second nature. It was then that I realised how much influence my childhood and family business had on me.

In 2009, our daughter, Jennifer, was two years old, and we realised that there were great possibilities in renting out bouncy castles and other paraphernalia for kiddies' parties. So what did we do? We started a party rental company. Once again, you may ask, what did I know about a rental business? The truth is: nothing! But I figured out that if I could give my best customer service to this new business that maybe, just maybe, it could be successful! And it was. Within six months, the business paid for itself.

Eighteen months later, I realised I had other dreams. I wanted to pursue a future on the stage as a Professional Speaker. However, I didn't have the time, so I decided to sell the rental business.

This time I didn't only sell the assets and clients, I shared my knowledge on customer service with the new owner, and within six months, she, too, had paid off the business and was successfully supporting her family by applying the simple techniques that I will share with you within this book!

Often, people ask me what inspired me and continues to inspire me to share my passion of customer service with audiences. I know first-hand that customer service has the power to change lives. The reason I know this is I was the recipient of exceptional customer service, and my life was irrevocably changed because of one individual's actions in a split second.

In October 2007, our baby girl, Jennifer, was born. Little did I know that just eighteen days later I would be left fighting for my life. I had been given an anti-inflammatory that had burnt a hole through my stomach and into the main artery running just beneath it.

On the 13th of November, with baby Jennifer a mere 18 days old, I was lying in a medical theatre surrounded by doctors and nurses. At 08:16 am on that fateful day, my time of death was called.

I had severely haemorrhaged, and my body was simply unable to cope.

The doctor in charge looked down at me, thought of my husband and my new baby, and something told him to fight for my life — and he did. An ordinary man who took an extraordinary chance on me resulted in my life being saved that day. In essence, I should have been sent off to the morgue, yet that doctor fought in the moments that mattered most, and for that I am so grateful.

This book is dedicated to people who in their own ways have been monumental in making my dreams come true:

To my parents, Bill and Mary Harrop, who gave me the most solid grounding I could ever have asked for when it comes to customer service.

To my brother, Sam, for always being on the other end of a Skype call.

To my amazing husband, Leonard, whose support has been unwavering.

To my two nieces, Amber and Leah-May, of whom we have guardianship, for their constant excitement at my progress.

To my two daughters, Jennifer and Amy, who I have the privilege of watching grow up.

And to a doctor who, under extraordinary circumstances, gave me the most exceptional customer service which is my biggest motivation to continue to share my message: a man who gave me my second chance at life — Doctor Dirk Pretorius.

Sarah Bauling

1
Convenience

When it comes to purchasing a product or service, something that is often considered is the convenience: the convenience of your customers finding the time to get to you, the convenience of your location, and the convenience of your operating hours.

Many years ago, we had two small dogs, Zorro and Zeta. I often thought about sending them to the doggy parlor for a monthly wash and cut. The only problem was time: finding the time to take them, not just now and again, but consistently every month.

By sheer luck, I found a local gentleman, Prince, who, as he put it, 'brought the doggy parlor to you!'. All I had to do was open the gate and let him and his team in. This, for me, was so convenient that I signed a contract right away.

Our two dogs grew to four, then five, and eventually six. Every time a new canine was added to the mix, Prince (the groomer) would add an extra 15 minutes per dog and add an extra amount to the monthly bill.

The truth is, with six dogs, I would probably get a pretty good rate at the doggy parlor up the road. However, for me, the cost in time, effort, and energy to get the dogs to the parlor up the road was not even comparable to the convenience of having Prince arrive, groom, and leave.

Every year, Princes' grooming fee goes up a small percentage; I don't even question it. Of course, because our dogs are groomed regularly, they always look beautiful. Neighbours have rung our bell to ask who grooms our dogs, and without fail, I share his details each and every time.

Apart from the fact that it is convenient for me, the dogs love Prince, and the moment he arrives, they are there to greet him! When it comes to exciting and delighting his clients, Prince certainly achieves that with the dogs!

I have definitely become a loyal, raving fan simply because it is so convenient for me to use his services.

If you look at your business, do you make it convenient for your customers to do business with you? Do you have a business that enables you to take your business to the client? If not, is your location ideal and easily accessible?

What are your operating hours? Does this suit the majority of your customers? What can you do to make it more convenient for your customers to do business with you and become your loyal, raving fans?

2
Creating A Comfortable Buying Environment

The environment in which your customers find themselves can be a big determining factor on whether they buy from you or buy from someone else.

Most children hate the dentist and love the hairdresser. I was different. I loved the dentist and hated the hairdresser.

My dentist had brightly coloured walls with a 'Jungle Story' mural. He had all sorts of paraphernalia hanging from his dentist light, and the waiting room was filled with fun toys.

My hairdresser had basins that were too high, which hurt my neck. The water was always way too hot, and the brushes they used were for 'big people's hair' and hurt.

When I look back, I think it is amazing how one guy, the dentist, got it so right, and the other, the hairdresser, got it so wrong!

In South Africa, we have a chain of amazing hair salons that cater for children. They're called 'Chop it'! My daughter loves 'Chop It', and the reason is simple; they have created a comfortable environment.

The walls and ceiling are filled with murals, and the chairs are high with lots of cushions so that the children are practically lying down for their hair wash, as opposed to stretching their little necks awkwardly to get their hair wet.

When they sit in front of the mirror, they have a TV playing cartoons and wrapped around their necks are either pink or blue clothing protectors.

Now you may be thinking that kids who go to 'Chop It' must be spoilt brats, but I have to tell you, as a mother and the person who pays the bill, I will choose 'Chop It' over any other salon. My little one is relaxed, which means I can catch up on some work or read a book as opposed to having to spend my time constantly calming her down. And what's even better is the price is the same as a regular salon. Now, I don't know about you, but for me, the environment makes sense for a child (and the mom!).

Let's take an adult environment like a retail store:

What music is playing?

- Is it so loud that you can't hear yourself think let alone hear what the sales consultant has to say?
- If you are based in a shopping mall where

customers are likely to have shopping trolleys, do the trolleys fit easily through the aisles of your store, or do your customers need to squeeze past one another?

If people phone your business, what music do you have while they're on hold?

- Is it annoying, relaxing, or upbeat?
- If your music-on-hold is linked into a local radio station, is it a station that is likely to be enjoyed by your clientele and target market. Is it appropriate?
- When you are speaking to clients on the phone, is there background noise that tells the person on the other end that you may not be able to hear them, or is there a gentle buzz of activity?

Your environment and buying space can make or break how a customer feels about your business, and this will be a determining factor on whether they come back or not.

A comfortable buying space has the power to create loyal, raving fans who will return time and time again just because it 'feels good'.

3
What Options Do You Offer?

I often ask people 'When was the last time you received exceptional customer service? What was it that made it so outstanding?' The answer is so simple: people like to be given options.

I guess it boils down to customers and potential customers wanting to know what options are available and what the benefits are relating to each of these options.

Take banking as an example; we want to know what account types are available; what benefits we get with these options; where do we get the best interest rates and best returns on our investments? We want to know that we are not just another client, but that the package we have chosen is as tailor-made as it can be for us. Let's face it; an 18-year-old student has very different banking needs to a CEO of a large corporation. The question is: 'Are there options in that bank for these two very different and individual people?'

There's a pretty good chance that there are, and this is where the people on the front line need to know and understand what the various options and benefits are.

Why would you want to pay for services you may never need? It's important to ensure that whoever is in the hot seat dealing with customers knows what the options are: all the ins and outs, the advantages and benefits.

At Bill Harrop's 'Original' Balloon Safaris, we were, in essence, selling the most memorable, amazing experience of hot-air ballooning. We learnt that, even in a market as niche as ours, customers still wanted options.

We found that most of our clients were celebrating special occasions, and although it was an expensive experience, they were prepared to pay. By listening to the customers who didn't purchase from us, we discovered another type of client: those that were keen on the experience of flying high yet weren't interested in the 'extra frills' such as breakfast, a certificate, and the bubbly.

And so, we created a second product: one that offered these clients the very thing they were looking for — a balloon flight only.

We increased our passenger numbers by simply having this option available.

You may wonder if we lost clients from our 'all the bells and whistles brand' to our 'no frills experience', and the answer is no! The reason we didn't lose clients is because those that wanted to spend more for the full experience did just that. We managed to gain customers by offering something that serviced a particular market need.

How does this relate to customer service? By being able to offer different options, it meant that our door was open for all types of customers. Naturally, we would offer our 'Bill Harrop' option first, yet the moment we were met with resistance, we were able to offer something they couldn't refuse!

So when it comes to your business, ask yourself these questions:

- What options do we have within our organisation?
- Are they clearly defined / packaged?
- Are the people who are on the front line knowledgeable on all options?
- Can your frontline staff confidently up sell, down sell and cross sell without confusing your clients with a slew of irrelevant information to ensure the client gets what will suit them best?

People want well focused options. They want to be able to choose. The moment they are able to do this, you have created a loyal, raving fan.

4
Keep Your Client In The Loop

Customers like to be kept in the loop from the moment they contact your business as a potential client right through to the final delivery.

So what do you need to do in order to provide exceptional customer service?

- Advise your clients on what they need to do.
- Advise them what you are going to do.
- Keep them informed and updated on any intermediate contingencies, i.e. airline and train delays.

Each business will differ; some will be more complicated than others. Retail (for example) is pretty simple: they arrive; they shop; they pay; and they leave. Sure, there is a whole deal more to the 'customer experience', which is covered in various chapters of this book. However, the system is relatively uncomplicated.

So for the purposes of this exercise, let's use a service

provider, such as a travel agent, as an example.

What does the client need to do?

In order to confirm a reservation, the system may require a deposit or full pre-payment within a defined time frame.

By simply advising your client of this, they are in the loop in terms of what is required for them to receive their confirmation.

You need to ask yourself, 'What does my client need to do so I can provide them with the best possible service?'

Make a list of what you need to tell them, so they can simply do it!

- The deposit amount?
- How it should be paid?
- Banking details / Credit card processes?
- When it should be paid?
- What to do once the payment has been processed, e.g. send a proof of payment?
- Where the proof of payment should be sent?
- What will happen once they have sent the proof of payment?
- What do you need to do?

This is a two-way street. By following the process, you can keep the client in the loop, which makes their dealing with you easy. Your client should never be thinking 'What now?'

Does the client need to be advised that the booking is made but can only be confirmed once the relevant deposit has been processed?

If you are dealing with your customers by telephone, you need to send something through to them in writing once the call has been concluded. You'll need to send this in writing because some people don't listen, they may have been distracted, or perhaps they didn't have a pen handy. By taking a few moments to send it through in writing, you have made it easy for them to 'do their bit'. (Tick for great service!)

Next, one of two things will happen—either they will pay, or they won't.

If they do not pay, you can follow up a day or two later with a simple 'I haven't seen the proof of payment come in as yet. I just want to make sure you've received the bank details?'

Why is this important? Why must you follow up with them? It shows you care. If they need to cancel, you have the opportunity to find out why and potentially salvage the situation. If they haven't received the banking details, you can resend them. Also bear in mind that, 'Proof of posting is not proof of delivery', so acknowledgement, even in the simplest form of a 'read receipt' is vital.

Once they have done their bit and paid, you can then

do what you promised and send them their confirmation.

By staying in touch with your clients and by advising them along the way, it ensures that they are always in the loop, and this avoids any frustration that may arise.

As business operators, we're there to serve our clients. No matter what, we should be making it as easy as possible for them to do business with us. Sure, it is up to them to play their part in the process. However, they are still the client no matter what, and without them, your business cannot survive.

By taking the time to get them in the loop and keep them in the loop, you create loyal, raving fans who never need to ask, 'What now?'

5
Ask

In order to be able to deliver exceptional customer service, it is vital to get certain information from your customer or potential customer.

The only way to get this information is to ask!

It is important to ask questions that will establish exactly how you can best assist your clients, how you can enhance their buying experience, and ensure that you consistently meet your clients' expectations. Asking questions also enables you to identify areas in your business where you may be able to improve. To get these answers, simply ask questions before, during, and after the sale.

As an example, I'd like to share some of the questions we asked our bouncy castle clients, the reasons why we asked them, and what we did with the answers.

1) In South Africa, the size of gardens varies vastly. Some folk live in townhouse complexes where space is limited, others have gardens that are as large as three, four, or even five hectares.

The bouncy castles we had in our portfolio came in various sizes from 3 x 3 meters right the way up to 7 x 7 meters. So as you can imagine, the last thing we ever wanted was to arrive and discover the castle booked was too big for the garden. To avoid this potential 'disaster', we needed to ask the right questions.

To back track for a moment; you may wonder why I used the word 'disaster'! The reason I use the word 'disaster' is because I can guarantee your attempts at explaining to a five-year-old that the castle mommy promised won't be here because it's too big will most likely land up in tears and a very, very sad little soul!

And so, in the bouncy castle business, one of the first and most important questions we asked was 'How big is your garden?'

Asking questions enables you to quickly lay a strong foundation for the rest of your dialogue, such as which bouncy castles would be suitable and whether we had suitable stock available for their requested dates.

2) Another way to exceed your clients' expectations and deliver fantastic customer service is to assess what else they may need based on what your main product offering is.

In the bouncy castle business, we realised that there was a big chance that if the client needed a bouncy castle, they may also need things like small chairs and tables, plastic plates and cups, and of course, there was always the cake! We added these items to our offering and ensured that, once we had secured a bouncy castle, we asked them if these were things they might need.

The results were astounding! Most clients 'hadn't thought about it' and were grateful for the suggestions. Of course, they were delighted that what started as a bouncy castle order ended up being their one-stop shop! The bonus for us is we had the opportunity of adding another 'item line' to their invoice!

3) Once a client has paid, had the product delivered, and all is done and dusted, it is often easy to happily move on. However, when it comes to delivering exceptional customer service, the 'after sale ask' is one of the most important sets of questions.

It is at this point that you can be the service provider who has gone the extra mile.

Ask your client if they were satisfied. Send your client an email or make a telephone call. Ask if their expectations were met and if they were satisfied. One of two things will happen:

Either they will be happy, which is great—you can keep on doing what you did.

Or they were not 100% satisfied. This is when you have the opportunity of making amends and learning where you, your product, and your company can innovate and improve.

In summary:

- Asking the right questions from the get-go allows you to establish what the client needs and how you are able to best assist them.
- Asking if they need extra products that relate to your main product offering gives you the opportunity of making your clients' lives easier, and it gives you the opportunity to make more money.
- Asking your clients if they were satisfied enables you to stay on track, or if need be, see how you can innovate to improve your product, experience, or service.

6
Would You Want To Do Business With You?

Good Question! Many people never think this way about the customer service they deliver.

When you sit back and have a good think about this question, you may immediately say 'Yes, I would', which is great. Now ask yourself why would you want to deal with you?

Is it because you are friendly? Helpful? Knowledgeable about the product you sell? Are you always on top of the world, ready to serve fully with enthusiasm? Maybe you genuinely love your job? Maybe you don't, but you value it nevertheless?

Of course, the answers will differ from person to person. If your answer is 'No, I wouldn't want to deal with me', ask yourself why.

Is it because you're not in a good place? Do you find your job boring? Are you uninspired? Are you tired?

The harsh truth is that if you couldn't bear to do business with yourself, there's a good chance your customers wouldn't want to do business with you either!

If you wanted to do business with yourself, how can you inspire others around you to have the same attitude? Perhaps ask them the same question! 'Hey guys, would you want to do business with yourself?' Watch their responses!

If you wouldn't want to do business with yourself, you need to figure out why? What can you change? What can you fix? What can you do differently?

Life can be challenging at times; however, the one thing you can control is how you react and respond to those challenges.

You have the power to spring out of bed in the morning.

You have the power to move with purpose; to be enthusiastic; and to be the helpful, knowledgeable, individual who is going to go into the world and serve your customers fully.

So take the time to ask the powerful question that puts things into perspective very quickly, 'Would I want to do business with me?'

Would you be your own loyal, raving fan if you were your customer?

7
Be Prepared To Go The Extra Mile

You may never actually have to go the extra mile, but the fact that you are prepared to, is a key ingredient in creating loyal, raving fans.

It was September 2014, and there was great excitement in our home. Our beautiful white cat, Twinkles, was pregnant. We waited in anticipation for the big arrival, and when we got home on the evening of the 15th of September, we met her four gorgeous kittens.

Within a few days, she had developed mastitis, which meant there was the possibility of us having to hand rear her kittens with syringes and kitten formulae. On the very same day that Twinkles had been diagnosed with mastitis, I was admitted to hospital, which meant the normal 'busy-ness' of our lives now fell straight into my husband's lap. He was dashing between dropping children at school, running his business, coming to see me in the hospital, fetching the children from school, handling the children's extra murals, and keeping an eye on the kittens to ensure that should Twinkles be unable to feed, he was ready to assist with the syringe and kitten formulae. (And who says a man can't multitask!)

I will admit, I felt really sorry for him. So I called the vet who I had been using for over eighteen years to ask that if Twinkles did stop feeding was there any way we could drop the kittens at the clinic until I was out of the hospital: simply to take the pressure off Leonard. Our amazing vet, who I had supported for eighteen years said, 'No . . . ' This was followed by 'If you need me to pop by and check on Twinkles and the kittens, I can easily do it in between shifts, which means you don't have to pay for the overnight stay, and Leonard can focus on you and your recovery.' In essence, it would have been far easier for him to have had Twinkles and her litter at the clinic, and he would have made more money. Yet, he was prepared to go the extra mile to serve a long-standing customer of eighteen years by literally driving the extra mile to our home.

The great news is Twinkles somehow managed to continue feeding her kittens; I came out of the hospital; and the vet did not need to make a house call.

Would I ever consider changing vets? No way!

Again, the lesson is that you may never actually have to go the extra mile, but the fact that you are prepared to do so is a key ingredient in, not only creating loyal, raving fans, but it's also a key ingredient in keeping loyal, raving fans as well!

8
Listen To Customer Complaints

When it comes to complaints, the customer ultimately wants the problem to be resolved, and you ultimately want the customer to leave happy!

Often, the hardest thing to do is listen to your customers, particularly when it's a complaint!

Have you ever complained and felt as if the person who is handling your complaint is so busy making excuses, not accepting accountability, or simply trying to stay out of trouble that they hear you but are not actually listening?

The obvious question is 'How are they ever going to fix this problem if they aren't listening to what I need?'

When it comes to an unhappy customer, they may be furious. By allowing them to vent and let off steam, they will eventually calm down.

If you listen during the vent, you will find that, most

often than not, they will make demands; they will say what they want in order for the issue to be resolved. The client may be calm when they complain. Again, they may make demands, and they may offer suggestions on how they feel the issue can be resolved.

By listening, you are able to identify what they want, and once you have this information, you are in a position to either resolve the issue yourself, or if need be, you are able to escalate it to someone who has the authority to sort it out.

If you are the person who handles complaints, I simply suggest you listen to what your customer is unhappy about as well as what they want you to do to make it right.

Let's take a retail store; if (for example) someone has bought a blouse, gone home, and discovered a stain, they'll usually bring it back to the store. They may demand to speak to a manager and demand that the blouse be replaced. If the manager is listening and understands that the way to make the customer happy is to replace the blouse, his work is done. The client has clearly said what they want. However, if the store manager is defensive, by the time he finally suggests that the blouse be replaced, which is what the customer wanted in the first place, the customer is usually exhausted and annoyed.

If you are faced with a complaint, your aim should be to identify what went wrong and how the customer would like the issue resolved.

Once you have listened, you are able to empathize. Tell the customer, 'Thank you for bringing this to my attention. Looking at this from your point of view, I too would probably complain. Let's see how we can sort this out for you.'

If you have listened to you customer's complaint, and by listening managed to empathize and resolve the issue, you are one step closer to creating a loyal, raving fan.

9
Make Sure Your Middle Man Keeps His Word

We live in a world of so many false promises.

Have you ever bought something from a social buying site? In 2012, I decided to spoil my family with a cruise. The terms and conditions (which boil down to the things they said they were going to do) were pretty clear. We would receive a confirmation within 72 hours. Imagine my surprise when 14 days later I had still not received the confirmation.

Being quite an avid cruiser, I knew that had I gone direct and paid direct I would have received the voucher within 72 hours; I knew that because I had done it several times before.

After many frustrating phone calls and emails and being put into an automatic system of 'Your call is important to us' day after day, I finally decided to 'get heavy' and go direct to the cruise company.

They explained how they were battling to get the money out of the social buying company, and that was why they were not able to send us our confirmation. From their side, they very simply needed the money in their bank account before they could confirm a booking.

The good news is, we did eventually get the confirmation.

There were a total of twenty-three emails sent: with two consultants and three managers having to handle my complaint. Do you have any idea how much time that is? When I look at that, I just think 'Wow! If they spent more time being efficient and less time sorting out complaints, they could have had effective sales people selling, not handling a non-systemized procedure and having a pretty mad client: Me!'

The net result of them having to 'bow' to their middle man resulted in this:

- Due to the inefficiency, I didn't ask anyone else to join us; the last time we had cruised, we had convinced 26 people to come along too!
- I would not use that social buying company again. In fact, I unsubscribed shortly afterwards.
- And when I cruise again, I will probably look for another cruise company.

Although they won this time around (since we paid and went and had a great time), in terms of being a repeat client, those chances are long gone! The six cruises we did beforehand where they had won me as a loyal, raving fan were blown simply because they used a middle man who hadn't looked after me.

Had the terms and conditions stipulated something they had been able to fulfil, it might have been a different story, but 72 hours is 72 hours!

The questions you need to ask are: 'Who are the middle men in your business?' Identify them.

'Are they making promises that you may not be able to keep?' If they are, my suggestion is that you come down on them fast and hard.

You may need a middle man in your business but don't be afraid to be selective of who that middle man is. The last thing you want is to lose a loyal, raving fan due to the middle man making a promise that can't be kept.

10
Make It Memorable

One of my favorite sayings is 'People may not remember what you did, but they will always remember the way you made them feel.'

Whether they felt good or bad, your customers are going to remember it. Kinesthetic memory outlasts all other kinds.

My recommendation is simple: make them feel good. Let their lingering memories of dealing with you, your company, or your product be positive.

Making it memorable can be about the simplest things: a friendly smile, a happy attitude, giving your time, and accepting that they may not be buying now but may be buying later. You should be setting out to help them and guide them and make them feel good, even when there may be nothing in it for you. These are the people that clients and potential clients remember, and when it comes to buying, these are the people they are likely to spend their money with!

Apart from the satisfaction of making other people feel great, when it comes to them remembering how you made them feel, here are three reasons why you as an individual, company, or product should be memorable to deal with:

- **As an individual** - be memorable to deal with. How do you know if you have achieved this? Simple. Your potential customers remember your name when calling back or returning to your store. Why is this important? If you work on commission, and you have done the work for a sale, and the client buys later from whomever else happens to answer the call or greet them on the store floor, you will miss out. If this happens, then you are to blame. It must be your priority to be so great to deal with that people ask for you by name.
- **As a company** - be memorable to deal with. People shop around, and there's a strong chance they'll be comparing you to others. What do they measure you against? Price? Quality? Longevity? You know who your competitors are and what they offer, and if you don't, you need to find out! The truth is that when you take away all the nuts and bolts, you will probably find that it is 'much of a muchness' which means you can gain the competitive edge by being the one company that stands out. Make your customers feel good, be exceptional, and stand out.

- **Your product or service delivery** - needs to be memorable. Why is this important? Well, if people out there are using your product, service, or experience, then there are probably a lot more people who could also be using your product, service, or experience. If you provide your customers with an overall memorable experience, they will be talking about you, your company, or the person they dealt with during the sale. This creates awareness and ultimately has the power to increase sales.

The memories you want to create should be good. Customers who feel good about the way they were treated by your team, by your company, and by results your product delivers, are likely to remember you and will recommend you and your company to others. They'll become those loyal, raving fans who add so much value to your business.

11

The Unexpected Is What Delights Customers

Most customers have an expectation of the level of service they are going to receive when purchasing a product, service, or experience.

In January 2015, I decided to change the soft furnishings in our dining room and living area. This meant new curtains, a lot of them, and new cushions, even more of them!

Our first stop was a franchise store specializing in curtains and cushions.

Their shop was a mess. We managed to scratch around and found half the curtains we needed and half the cushions.

After having to ask them to check the stock on the computers and discovering we had managed to find all the curtains and cushions they had in stock, I had to request they phone another store within the franchise.

They called and established the other store had the stock I needed.

We left the store with six large bags, which meant two trips back and forth to the car and store. On arrival at the second store, we managed to find the curtains and cushions quickly and easily. As we packed the six large bags, the teller placed a sign that read 'please use the next teller' on her work station, then she grabbed three bags, smiled, and said, 'Let's get these to your car!'

I was blown away by her attitude, her desire to assist, and the fact that she did it on her own accord. As we made our way down to the car, she chatted to us and asked why we needed so many curtains and cushions, and when we told her, she seemed genuinely excited and commented on how beautiful the curtains and cushions would look together.

The first store did nothing wrong, yet they certainly did not go the extra mile. Their service was average. They did the bare minimum to get by and there were no unexpected surprises.

The second store, same franchise, had a teller who made the effort to assist us in carrying the large, heavy bags, and she made the effort to be enthusiastic about our purchase.

Would I return to store one? No! Would I return to store two? Absolutely, and I would have no problem in recommending them to anyone who asked.

The unexpected deed of assisting us in carrying our bags to the car was so small in the bigger picture, yet the impact was massive.

What are the unexpected surprises you can add to your customer service experience?

Often, it is the unexpected surprises that delight and excite your customers and create loyal, raving fans.

12
Serve Fully

What is customer service?

Customer service is what a client or potential client receives before, during, and after they purchase a product, experience, or service.

Have you ever been served by someone who is 'half there'? Someone who is just doing a job? How did that feel? Not great, right?

So the question I would like to pose to you is: 'How do you serve your customers?' My advice to anyone who deals with customers is to serve them without holding back, in other words, to serve your customers fully!

Two amazing things happen when you serve your customers fully.

First, if you are focused on your customer and potential customer, and your aim is to serve fully, you will be so engaged that the chances of them buying from you are pretty high. We know that without sales, we don't have a business, so although customer service is not always about sales, we need to remember that without customer service, you don't have the foundation on which to build sales, business success, and profitability.

By serving your customers fully, you are focused on them. You're not distracted by other things. Those other things could be stuff going on in your personal life, stuff that isn't work related, or simply things that distract you. In that moment, by being focused on your client, focused on positively serving them fully, you are creating a positive vibe and persona, and this will spill into all areas of your life.

A second amazing thing happens when you serve fully. Your customers are probably caught in the rush of life; they have their own set of problems (of which they are hoping you will be solving one of them), and who knows their circumstances and what stress they may have? By you serving fully, you are able to 'steal them from reality' – even if it is just for the few minutes that you get to deal with them.

You have the opportunity to make them feel like the most important person in the world: where the problem that they have brought in is as important to you as it is to them. You can literally make someone's day by serving him or her fully.

If your customers have a 'to do' list and your product is something that can get one of those items 'ticked off', don't just 'tick it off' for them, allow them to feel so important that they tick it off and have an amazing day!

Serving fully is about focusing, acknowledging, and assisting as best you can. It is ensuring that if you can serve them, you do, and if you cannot, they at least feel like you care enough to try.

By serving your customers fully, you increase your chances of closing the deal, and you will have the opportunity of simply making someone else's day.

13

Treat Every Client As If They Are Your Top Client

Do you have a list of your top clients? If you don't have this list, I strongly suggest you get it. You need to know who is bringing in the big bucks in your organization! You need to identify who your loyal, raving fans are!

Once you know who your top clients are, you can ask yourself these seven simple questions:

1. How do I treat them?
2. How do I speak to them?
3. How often do I contact them?
4. How do I contact them?
5. How do I thank them?
6. Who is dealing with them?
7. How can I get more 'top clients'?

When I looked at our family business, Bill Harrop's 'Original' Balloon Safaris, and asked myself these very questions, the answers were interesting. For us, we were selling a 'once in a lifetime experience' which, in essence, means most of our passengers were ultimately going to do this 'once in a lifetime'!

So who were our 'repeat clients' if folks were only going to do this once?

Who were the people who were using us time and time again?

The people who were using us time and time again were various travel agents and tour operators who would send their clients who were looking for their 'once in a lifetime experience'. Our top clients, our loyal, raving fans were these travel agents and tour operators.

When I took a step back and asked the seven vital questions, I got seven simple answers!

- We treated them well and with efficiency.
- We spoke to them with enthusiasm. In many cases, we had the advantage of having great rapport with them due to us having dealt with them so often.
- We generally liked to touch base with them at least once a month.
- If we hadn't heard from them over a period of a month, we picked up the phone, said 'hi', and asked if they needed anything! In your business, also consider phoning on birthdays and anniversaries, or if you hear news of their children's achievements or illnesses. Read their social media such as Facebook.

It shows you are interested in them. That's why people 'post': to keep interested people interested. Therefore, all you have to do is to let them know you care too.
- We had various ways of thanking our top clients. The easiest was simply saying 'thank you'. We would invite them to fly with us for their special occasion, for their own 'once in a lifetime experience'.
- In the tourism industry, commission is earned by travel agents and tour operators, so a simple phone call to advise them that their commission was paid is a great reason to touch base and advise them to look out for the 'ker-ching' in their bank account!
- We established who in our organization was predominantly dealing with our top clients. By establishing who was dealing with our top clients, we could establish what they were doing differently and how they were doing it. In doing this, we could identify how we could use these techniques throughout the organization, and this had an amazing two-fold effect: firstly, it inspired the staff members with whom the techniques were shared, and secondly, it inspired those who were doing an exceptional job to keep on doing it!

And before we get to question number seven, allow me to pause right here.

I'm sure you'll agree that getting the answers to

questions 1 - 6 is the easy part; however, doing something effective now that you have those answers is what will really make the difference in 'getting more top clients'.

The great news is that this is easier than most folks think!

Once we had established whom our top clients were and answered those six questions, we simply emulated what we did with our top clients with all our clients!

Top clients are the loyal, raving fans who return to your business time and time again; those who recommend your business to others; and the ones who you 'WOWed' with great service.

If you treat every person as if they are your top client, you have a far greater chance of them becoming just that!

14
P's And Q's

The Ps and Qs — the please and thank you's: those phrases that our parents drummed into us as children!

As life goes on, we use our Ps and Qs quite naturally, and then . . . (da da da dum - drum roll . . .) we start our professional lives!

Manners work two-fold when it comes to customer service. There are times when you are the service provider and times when you are the customer.

Let's start with the service provider. How often have you experienced a customer complaint? It may start quite nicely, but the moment the service provider gives them a hard time, the customer most likely kicks into demand mode and says things like 'I need to speak to your manager now. I demand that this is sorted out.'

Although the customer may well be within their rights, even if they are not but feel they are, it can result in the service provider not wanting to assist.

Now let's look at the customer — the customer who

quite simply remembers their manners will be met with assistance. As they say, for every action, there is a reaction, and manners illustrate this perfectly!

If you are the person who is on the other end of the line receiving the rude or irate customer, the best thing to do is remember your manners. Your manager may not be available, so being polite and calm is the only way to handle it! You could try something like 'The manager is not available at the moment. Please, can I get some details from you so I can get him to call you back with all the facts as soon as he is available?' This approach will have a far better response than 'The manager is not available.' What is the problem?'

As 'out of line as' the client may seem, it's important to remember that the last thing you want to do is add fuel to the fire.

Some useful sentences that you may be able to use:

> *'Thank you for your call and your concern.'*
>
> *'Please, can I try to assist you so I can escalate this.'*
>
> *'I am sorry your expectations were not met. Please let us try to make this right.'*
>
> *'Would you mind if I take a message so someone who can sort this out can get back to you?'*

All are gentle, yet effective.

The client's reaction will be dictated by how upset they are. However, if you start off politely, there's a much greater chance you will come to a mutually beneficial result.

Alternately, if you are the unhappy customer, no matter how the service provider treats you, or how good or bad their manners are, I can guarantee that if you persevere with good manners, you will get a far more favourable response and outcome.

And it's not only in the complaints department that manners matter. Good manners should apply throughout your entire operation.

When someone phones your office, how are they put on hold? Does the conversation go like this? 'Good morning, can I please be put through to Alice?' boom . . . and the call is transferred? Or do they get a moment of your receptionist's time for her to simply say 'Certainly, please hold.'?

And here is the final set of manners: 'Thank you' could be 'Thank you for using our service'; 'Thank you for buying our product'; or 'Thank you for coming into our store'. I'm sure you get it.

Oh, and while I have you, thank you for buying my book!

15

Sometimes The Client DOESN'T Want To Talk To You

When it comes to customer service, we often think it boils down to being on the end of every telephone line: being fully accessible at any given moment. For some people, this may ring true. However, there are others who simply find convenience the greatest customer service they could ask for.

Convenience is about the customer being able to get what they want when they want it. It could be that they simply want information, or alternately, they want to buy a product or service.

It is about being able to open a bank account or get comparative quotes on insurance online. It's about your customers being able to log onto a website and find the information they're seeking.

People do business with people, but people also want the efficiency and convenience that our technological world can offer. Many people are entirely happy predominantly dealing online and find any other commercial interaction inconvenient.

Now if you are 'old school', you may be going into cardiac arrest right now at the mere thought of putting your business online! You need to remember that this is how the world works these days! So deep breathe in and deep breathe out!

It doesn't mean that just because your business is 'online savvy' that you can kick all the staff out and run a big corporation on your own. You still need staff to answer your customers' queries, send more information, follow up, process, and more importantly; you need the people in your business for those of us who actually prefer dealing with people.

I am a people person. I would rather pick up the phone and dial the operator than send an email. My husband finds that dealing with operators is time consuming. He gets annoyed when he's transferred from one person to another. He's a perfect example of the consumer who would prefer to send an email.

However, whatever method of communication we choose, each of us expects it to be dealt with quickly and efficiently. In your business, you need to be prepared to handle both types of enquiries equally well.

Have your online option for those who find it convenient to open a bank account at midnight. Accept that many people perceive great customer service as simply being able to get the answers when they want them, even if a human is not the one giving the answers!

The questions to ask are:

- What does our company sell, or what service do we provide?
- Do we offer an online option?
- Is our website user-friendly?
- Is our website up to date?
- If someone purchases online, what guarantees do they have, and will it be delivered on time?
- Do we have the vital element of people in our business for those who prefer dealing directly?

The customer may not always want to talk to you; for some, exceptional customer service is about being able to do what they want when they want it. It's about being able to get the information here and now!

16
Get Feedback

What does feedback have to do with customer service? Everything! Feedback from past and current customers gives you the opportunity to see where your business is exciting and delighting customers. It also gives you the opportunity to see if there are areas where you are not meeting and exceeding your clients' expectations. Once you have that information, you're able to build on the positive and work on the areas that are falling short.

How often have you taken the time to follow up with a past or current customer: someone who has used your services before or someone who uses your services on a continuous or regular basis?

It's easy to become complacent, especially when business is ticking over.

It's easy to assume that your customers are happy because they are still using you.

It's easy to assume that clients have not used you again because they simply don't need your services now.

Although some or all of these statements may be true, be very wary of assuming anything.

Just as you may assume all is well, how about assuming all is not well?

How about assuming that your clients are using you until they find another supplier or find the time to change providers?

How about assuming that customers have not come back because they're unhappy?

If you looked at it like this, wouldn't you want to know:

- How you can ensure your clients DON'T go elsewhere and,
- How you can win back those lost clients?

So what can you do to ensure you're on track with your assumed loyal customers: the ones who could maybe use you more or are not doing business with you because you assume it is just that they don't need your services right now? Get feedback of course!

There are a couple of ways of doing this. One might work . . . one will definitely work.

You could send them an email, which they might get to when they have a moment. However, they usually won't make it a priority, so you may be wasting your time.

Alternately, you could physically ask them! It's always

harder for someone to 'get to it when they can' as opposed to being in an easy position to reply. If you are on the phone with them, there's good chance you will get your answer right away!

So try this. Pick up a phone and ask a current client 'How are you finding our service?'

Their reply may be a quick 'Excellent! Thanks for asking!' Which firstly makes them feel valued and secondly tells you unequivocally that they believe things are going well.

If this is their response, find out what blew their minds and take this into account when dealing with future customers. Build on this positive re-enforcement.

Alternately, you might hear something like 'I'm glad you called. Here are a couple of concerns . . .'

This is where the real value lies in a follow up. Your customer will give you insight that you may or may not have already had. It gives you the chance to hear what is going wrong in their eyes, and more importantly, it means you have the opportunity of putting it right before they stop using you. If one customer has a niggle, and if you can nip it in the bud there and then, think of the overall advantages this can have on your business.

Try stepping out of your comfort zone and calling the client who hasn't used you in a while. You might ask them, 'I see you haven't used our company since

January – is there anything I can assist you with now?'

They may tell you they simply haven't had a recent requirement for your products or services; nevertheless, this phone call makes them feel valued and shows you care. Alternately, the conversation might open your eyes to something you didn't realise or something they were unhappy about that could have encouraged them to look for a new supplier. By calling them, you may have a chance to win them back. If you can't win them back, you'll know what went wrong. It can be a lesson learned so you don't lose any other clients for the same reasons.

If your company has a 'Customer experience feedback form', how do you deal with the responses? Maybe you have seen these yourself in other businesses! Perhaps you stayed in a hotel and filled in a form before you checked out. How often have you given some constructive feedback?

I know I have done that many a time! And the next pertinent question is how often has anyone come back to you to either thank you for your feedback or come back to say they realised something was amiss in the system, and it is going to be rectified?

Now that I have never had!

If your company has a 'Customer experience feedback form', what are you doing with the information? Do you revert and thank your customers, or does it land up in some manager's desk drawer never to be seen again?

Be proactive and get feedback from past and current customers, but always make sure you are ready for the responses. Use the positive responses to reinforce what you are doing well and to motivate yourself, your staff and your colleagues. And when you get complaints or constructive criticism, thank them for their feedback and then do something about it.

Even if you are giving exceptional service, if you are doing everything right, don't become complacent. Always be ready to ask for and receive feedback.

If time is a resource that you wish you had more of – start with one feedback a day. By month-end, that will be twenty or thirty times more input than you had before. Imagine how much customer insight you will have gained and how much leverage this can give your business.

Feedback from clients, past and current, gives you the perfect opportunity to find ways to excite and delight your customers.

17
Make Exceptions

I am all for the processes and systems within a business. They're important. Businesses without well-organised systems often fail for just that reason.

But sometimes you need to break the rules. Sometimes you need to have a little flexibility. When delivering exceptional customer service, there are times when we need to make exceptions. Why? Because often, flexibility is that one step in the 'extra mile'.

In January 2013, my six-year-old daughter, Jennifer, was desperate to go for a pony ride. We were on holiday on the coast, and for her, this would have been the highlight of the trip.

We found a stable yard that offered pony rides an hour's drive away. With her big blue eyes and her 'Please Mommy', there was no way I could say no, so we hit the road.

We arrived at 14:30. The lady at reception told us the

last pony rides finished at 14:00, but we were welcome to take a walk up to the paddocks and look at the ponies.

Now if you have a six-year-old, looking at a pony and riding a pony are two very different things!

Anyway, we headed up to the paddocks and found a man untacking the horses.

I asked him if there was any way that Jen could have a five-minute lead walk on the pony. As a customer service guru, I could see that the groom, Bongani, wanted to say yes, but he knew the rules. He said 'Ma-am, I would love to say yes, but my boss is so strict; no pony rides after 14:00.' Jennifer's little face had tears pouring down it. She was so close yet so far.

Bongani looked at her, looked at me, and in a hushed voice said, 'Please go and ask my boss – he is over there.' Instead of taking the saddle off the pony, he walked off to do something else.

His boss ambled over and when I asked him, he glanced at the ponies and said, 'Well looks like your lucky day! Capri still has her saddle on. We usually don't do pony rides after 14:00, but it won't take longer than 10 minutes.'

This story illustrates two points when it comes to making exceptions:

The groom, Bongani, knew he didn't have the power to authorise an after-hours pony ride. He sent us to someone who did, and he deliberately made sure that Capri, the cute black pony, was still saddled up. He knew that if the saddle was off, there was no way his boss would say yes. Bongani knew that his boss would make the exception if he made it easy for him to do so.

The second point was the receptionist. There was no give, no flexibility. She could have picked up the phone and called the stable manager. Instead, she watched a little six-year-old who had been driven an hour for a ten-minute pony ride being totally crushed. She was the 'Rules Chick', but Bongani was 'The guy who made it happen'.

Making an exception may involve a little extra time or effort on your side, but the look on a child's face might just make it all worthwhile.

On our next holiday, would I drive an hour for Jen to ride a pony at those stables again? Absolutely yes!

When it comes to your business and your company, be 'the guy who makes it happen'.

Don't be afraid to see how you can be flexible when it comes to the rules and processes and see where you can 'give a little' and how this 'give and flexibility' can excite and delight your customers.

18
Be Helpful

Being helpful can be the clear differentiator between the success and failure of a business.

If customers or potential customers knew the answer to their requirement, they wouldn't be asking for help. So it's your duty to help them. It sounds obvious, so why do so many businesses overlook it and fall short?

If you are the retail business and a customer approaches you or one of your staff looking for something - do you haphazardly point in the general direction of where they might find it, or do you walk with them to the right department to assist them in finding it? And if you can't find it, do you take the time to check on the computer system to see if it's in stock? If you don't have stock and you are part of a franchise, do you make the effort to track down the item elsewhere?

You may be thinking, 'Whoa! Slow down! That's a lot of effort for just one customer!'

I suggest you ask yourself these two questions!

1. If this customer were your only customer, would it then be too much effort?
2. If this single customer were the difference between breaking even and losing money that week, would it still be too much effort?

Of course, there is always the chance that you are super helpful and still don't get the sale this time. However, what you have done is set yourself up for next time.

If you have served that one customer as if your business depended on it, if you've been helpful and tried to assist them, it is you that they will remember the next time they're in the market for whatever you're selling!

No matter what business you're in, if you deal with customers in any way whatsoever, you're operating a Customer Service Department. You're there to service your customers, to answer their 'silly questions', to guide them through their queries, and to help them find the answers they are looking for.

Remember, a 'silly question' is not silly to the person who asks it. Maybe they are embarrassed to ask and may say, 'Perhaps this is a silly question, but . . . ', and your response should be, 'There is never such a thing as a silly question, but there is such a thing as a silly answer. So, let me do my best to give you a sensible answer.'

Remember, exceptional customer service is not just

about the sale; customer service is also about 'after the sale'.

If a customer comes back with a query, a complaint, or a concern, are you there to assist them and make their total buying experience great?

- Do you assist them with their query?
- Do you effectively handle their complaint?
- Do you ease their concerns by explaining things?

Never hold back from doing everything you possibly can to help a customer. Most of the time, helping a customer requires very little effort. The times when you'll need to move heaven and earth for a customer may happen once in a blue moon, but it's the 'once in a blue moon customer' who will come back time and time again. It will be this customer who will become your loyal, raving fan!

19

You Never Know WHO Your Customer REALLY Is!

Our daughter Amber was 18 years old and fresh out of high school! She came home with her head held high to announce that she had found a job. It was perfect: near home, a small cake store that had a variety of walk-in and telephone customers, and a pretty good vibe.

However, a few months later the reality of 'Horrible Bosses' hit home. She was constantly demotivated from being shouted at; she was tired of continually being blamed for others' errors; and the thought of facing her boss, who constantly smelt of booze, was enough to send her over the edge.

Amber had gotten to the stage where she really didn't enjoy working at the cake store, yet somehow she dragged herself there with a great attitude every day, even though she often came home crying!

She decided to look for a new job and within two days had an interview set up.

Her interview for the new position was set for an evening, and on the day of her interview, a man walked into the store with whom Amber ended up spending almost an hour. As a result, she made a pretty big sale; in fact, the biggest sale that month. As she cheerfully waved him goodbye, her horrible, boozy boss summoned her to his office. He wasn't happy that she had spent so much time with one customer, calling it 'unacceptable'. She was at a loss for words. First of all, no one else had been in the store, she had three colleagues on the floor, and of course, there was the little matter of the biggest sale of the month!

She headed off to her interview that evening, and halfway through the discussion, the lady running the interview apologized; the big boss was unable to make the interview and wanted to Skype into the meeting. Imagine Amber's surprise when the man on the screen was none other than the one she'd assisted in the cake store just a few hours earlier!

Of course, she got the job! Why? He took one look at her and said 'I liked your attitude today! And you're a pretty good sales person too.'

Amber was in such a bad place at work, yet somehow she managed to rise above it; she managed to focus on her clients despite the fact that she had broken the fifteen-minute rule. She'd been treated like a doormat but never took her eye off the most important thing in the business: the client! She may have lost that particular battle with her boozy boss, but she definitely won the war!

What is the moral of the story? You just never know who your client is. They could be nobody; they could be anybody; they could be somebody who will take you and your business to new heights. Always make your customer your number-one priority; you just never know who they are!

20

Treat People As You Would Like To Be Treated!

I attended a Catholic school run by nuns.

One lesson that always stood out for me was to treat others the way you would like to be treated.

I have no idea how the nuns managed to get that into my head, but I do know it is an indelible memory! I managed to take this small affirmation with me right through school and into my business life, and it is something I've always found very useful.

For example, when someone calls your business to ask for a reference on a staff member, how are they dealt with? Patience or impatience?

When a life insurance company calls to sell life insurance, do you feel irritated, or do you empathize with them for the difficult job they need to do?

When someone phones your company to update their records, do you fob them off, or do you give them the two minutes they need to do their job?

When a mobile phone company calls to try to sell you a new tariff or network, how do you respond?

I'm not saying that you should grant oodles of time to each and every person who calls to sell you something, or that you shouldn't respond if you're not interested in order to save them and yourself the time. What I am suggesting is that you respect people equally. Understand that they are trying to do their jobs and make a living, and you just happen to be part of their daily plan. Dealing with everyone with patience, empathy, respect, and time may take a little effort, but the effects are awesome.

Imagine yourself in their shoes and someone tells you to get knotted. It might not ruin your day, and you'd probably be used to it if you were doing that job, but it wouldn't be positive or memorable. The memorable person is the one who politely declines, who thanks them for taking the time to call, and courteously informs them they are not interested.

Every time you encounter an annoying client or phone call, take a moment to think: if that were me on the other end of the line, how would I like to be treated?

The courtesy you grant them may make their day, even if you're not buying from them, and you won't have gotten yourself worked up. Let them know about your business and make sure they know what you do. Every inbound call is an opportunity. In the future, if they are ever looking for what you provide, they may just call you because you were probably one of the few people who was courteous and polite!

Leave people feeling good. You win and they win, and to be honest, it's a lot easier to be pleasant than it is to be impatient, irritated, and rude!

You may be wondering how this relates to customer service? Simply put, you never know who your next client is, and what influence they may have. If you treat everyone with respect, kindness and empathy, and treat people as you would like to be treated, you will reap the rewards down the line.

21
What Does Your Client Actually Need?

How often have you found yourself being given advice from a sales consultant and thought 'This is all fine and well, but this is not relevant to me?'

When it comes to products, experiences, and services, it is vitally important to understand that one client's needs are likely to differ from another clients needs – people often have different requirements.

As an example, Bill Harrop's 'Original' Balloon Safaris has a fleet of six balloons from a small two-man balloon right through to the largest balloons that carry up to 18 passengers each. Ballooning is an experience that appeals to a wide range of potential clients from romantic engagements right through to large corporate team-building days.

One of the first questions we asked any potential client was: 'Is this for a special occasion?' Based on the answer, we saw how best to assist them. A romantic balloon safari for two is very different than a corporate adventure for a hundred. By knowing what the occasion was and how many passengers were in the group, we were in a position to give them what they were looking for.

For the happy couple, we focused on the romance and special extras. For corporate groups, we focused on the fun, team-building aspects.

By asking your client pertinent questions you are able to avoid confusion and keep focused on what the client does want, as opposed to what he doesn't. If you give every single client the same information regardless of what they want, you will overload them with information. They will be confused, and the truth is an overloaded, confused client rarely buys!

You may be thinking, 'This sounds like sales not customer service!' I will agree in one sense that, yes, it's about using the correct sales dialogue. However, customer service is about giving your customers and potential customers information that enables them to make an educated decision. If they have the relevant information that meets their criteria, you will not have to sell. They will buy because the product, experience, or service is exactly what they are looking for.

Customers become loyal, raving fans when they are able to purchase a product, service or experience that fulfills their needs.

22
Motivation

There's no better feeling than being motivated, whether it's to do something, to achieve a goal, or to be able to press on no matter what stands in your way.

There is also no better feeling than being around a motivated individual: someone who is so fired up that you can't but help find yourself being reeled in and ignited by their energy!

When it comes to customer service, motivation can be had and shared by so many people. It could be you, your colleagues, your boss, or your customer.

If you are motivated, it is so contagious that everyone around you will feel driven as well: driven to sell, driven to support, driven to succeed, and driven to buy.

So, are you motivated? What motivates you? You may be wondering what does 'being motivated' have to do with customer service and creating loyal, raving fans?

You may be motivated to succeed with your customers

because you rely on commission. Perhaps you are motivated because you know you are enhancing your customers' lives. Whatever it is, seek it out and make it your driving force.

If you see your colleagues are 'not in the groove', motivate them with positive words; avoid the in-house dramas that happen in companies — the water-cooler or smoke-rooms chats.

If you are motivated for the right reasons, your customers will feel it, and there's a good chance they will be motivated to buy from you.

If there are other companies selling what you are selling, don't be afraid to motivate your clients to buy from you. If they say no, ask why? They will appreciate the fact that you care enough to ask. If their reason is one that you can solve, tell them about it. Motivate them to change their mind and choose you or your company.

Motivation to buy is not always about price. It's often about the attitude of the person who is selling or promoting the product or service.

Do you remember the last time you were at a restaurant? Perhaps you looked through the menu and chose something. The waiter arrived at your table with the list of 'Todays Specials'. His job is to motivate you to choose something that's not on the menu. He has been motivated by the chef or the manager. If he's enthusiastic, there's a good chance you may consider trying it!

The motivation from the chef passes to the waiter, and this passes onto you, the customer.

When it comes to your business, before you start your sales dialogue, ask yourself:

- Am I motivated about the product or service I'm providing?
- Am I excited about what I can offer potential clients?
- What is motivating me?
- Are you motivating those around you by being enthusiastic?
- If not, why not?

Change your mindset if necessary and figure out what you can do to become motivated to sell more and serve your customers fully.

- Do your customers need a little push, a little more enthusiasm, or a little motivation from you as to why they should choose you above someone else?
- Do they feel your excitement and enthusiasm?
- Is your motivation from the heart? Do you really believe your product, service, or experience will change or enhance your customers' lives?

And after the sale or liaison ask yourself;

- How did it feel?

- Was it a success?
- Is the client happy, satisfied, excited, and delighted?

And if you can answer yes, does this not motivate you to do it again? If so, then you are heading in the right direction.

Some people are born with motivation, and others have to work hard to get it. The amazing thing about motivation is once you are feeling it, it will drive you in unimaginable ways. Not only will you be satisfying your clients and inspiring those around you in the workplace, but the motivation you feel will spill into your personal life, and this will positively affect everyone around you.

Find what motivates you and allow it to continually inspire you to do the best and be the best you can be. Your customers will feel it, and in turn, will become loyal, raving fans.

23
Maximize

Maximizing is about ensuring your customers get the most out of your product, experience, or service.

The great thing about maximizing is that you are specifically looking at customers who have already purchased from you—customers who are currently using your services.

You may be thinking 'Why do I need to spend time on these folks since they're already on board?'

It takes seven times as much time, effort, energy, and money to gain a new client than it does to keep the ones you already have. This is why it is worth looking after and keeping the customers who are using your products and services! This is why, if there is any way that your clients can get the most out of your product, you need to ensure they do!

A good friend of mine, Desi, travelled to India in December 2014. Her travel agent ensured that she had everything in order: from air tickets to hotel accommodation; from visas to forex; and of course made sure she had travel insurance. The agent also advised her to let the credit card company know she would be travelling overseas, which Desi duly did.

In February 2015, Desi received her new credit card, and on reading through the documentation, discovered that as a 'Private Banking Client' (which she had been for many years), one of the advantages was free travel insurance. Funny enough, when she should have been jumping for joy, she was irritated! She had spent a few thousand rand on travel insurance when she could have actually had it for free!

So, who did not maximize her experience? The travel agent could have suggested that she check with her bank, yet the blame, in my opinion, fell squarely on her bank. Free travel insurance was an advantage of banking with them, yet she didn't know about the benefit. When she called her bank to advise them that she was travelling overseas, it would have been the ideal opportunity for the consultant to ask her if she knew she could get free travel insurance, as well as assist her in processing it.

Had the bank done this, not only would she have saved money, but they would have created a loyal, raving fan simply because she had received an 'unexpected extra'.

When it comes to your customers repurchasing, renewing, or recommending your product, service, or experience, it is the unexpected extras, the things that have maximised their experience, that can be the differentiating factor of them using you or someone else.

So when it comes to your business:

- What are the unexpected extras you can offer your customers?
- How can you maximize your customers' experience?
- Do all of your staff know what these extras are and how to redeem and process them?

Maximizing a customer's experience ensures that they stay and recommend you to others. It is one of the easiest ways to create loyal, raving fans!

24
Who Is Accountable?

There are times in any business when the waters get rough, and the client's query or problem needs to be escalated.

There are two types of people in any business: those that can make decisions, and those that cannot.

If you are in the first category, those that can, you need to ask yourself these questions:

- Do I have an open-door policy?
- If someone has a problem that needs to be resolved and they are not in a position to make a decision, am I available to assist them?

There are only two potential answers to these questions — yes or no!

If it's yes, then you are on the right track. If it is no, this is not a train smash by any means, but then the questions I have for you are these:

- If a staff member makes a decision that you don't agree with, are you prepared to back them on it?
- Who is accountable and responsible, and can they make a business decision in your absence?
- Is there a defined decision-making process in your company?

Your staff or team may have stumbling blocks from time to time. If they are in a position to ask someone for assistance, it means they can be confident in making the customer experience great. That someone could be you, it could be the person you have put in charge to make decisions, or it could even be the very staff member who is handling the query. As long as everyone knows where the buck stops, they have somewhere to go if they have a question or query. If they have no one to turn to, then you, as the person who can make decisions, need to support your staff at critical times.

If you are in the second category, the 'cannot make decisions' category, ask yourself:

- What am I accountable for in my role in this company?
- If I have a question, who do I go to?

It is vital that you know your accountability level in your work environment so you can confidently make a decision when required.

By knowing who to go to when something needs to be escalated, you will have the confidence to serve your customers without fear of getting things wrong, making a mistake, or making a bad judgment.

Don't be afraid to ask for help, and don't be afraid to be the one who can offer the support when needed.

It's vital to know who is accountable for what so you and your team can serve your customers fully, and in doing so, create loyal, raving fans.

25
I Can't Do It!

Great customer service is sometimes about having the courage to turn business away simply because it's not your area of expertise.

When I first invested and rented out properties, one of my biggest bugbears was trying to find a handyman who was reliable, delivered good-quality work, and was affordable. I eventually found a Polish couple, Monika and John. Although their English was almost non-existent, they ticked all three boxes: they pitched up on time every time, did an excellent job, and their rates were reasonable.

They did various jobs over the years for me from painting and tiling right through to installing electrics and laminate flooring.

I called them one day to have a look at a wall that had developed damp, and as they looked at it they chatted in Polish. Monika eventually said to me that she could do the job but would suggest we find someone else. Through her rather broken English, she eventually managed to say that although they could do it and charge less than an expert, she would rather recommend someone who specialised in damp. They may charge more but would be able to offer a guarantee that she couldn't.

I know they really needed the money because she was always 'looking for more jobs' as she put it, yet they were prepared to pass a job on to someone else simply because she did not want to let me down.

Although I found Monika rather difficult to understand — generally a two-minute conversation between her English and my lack of polish took about fifteen minutes — I trusted her. To this day, whenever I get a new tenant, I hand them the lease as well as her business card. If my tenants need any repairs done, I advise them to call Monika directly. Occasionally, I receive an invoice via email. After a quick call to the tenant to make sure all is in order, I pay it. No mess, no fuss.

The reason I have so much trust in them boils down to the day of the damp in the wall and the fact that she had the courage to say no. That 'No' strengthened my belief in her and that they would always, without fail, let me know if they were called for a job they couldn't do.

Monika and John have never ripped me off. They arrive when my tenants call, they consistently do a good job, their rates are fantastic, and from time to time, I get a 'broken English' telephone call to say the job is too big, too complicated, or requires a real expert to fix. She has managed to instil such trust in me simply because she has the courage to say no when she knows she can't do a brilliant job.

Do you know exactly what you do and what you're good at?

Do you have the courage to pass the job onto someone else who can deliver what you can't?

Although you may lose a job from time to time, by being honest and not over promising and under delivering, you are able to create loyal, raving fans.

26
Smile

How does a smile relate to customer service? Well, quite simply, a smile can change the way a person feels. It can create the impression of how your client or potential client perceives you and your business, and both of these can be the final convincing factor on whether a potential client will purchase from you.

A smile is the simplest thing in the world, yet the reaction to a smile can change a world. It could change your world or your customers' world.

If you're in retail, dealing face-to-face with prospective buyers, a smile is the one thing you must have. There's a Chinese proverb that says, 'A man who doesn't smile mustn't open a shop.'

Who wants to buy from someone who is grumpy and miserable? I don't know about you, but I don't want to buy from them, no matter what they are selling and no matter how badly I need it!

A smile leads to a friendly face that gives the appearance that you are interested in your client and want them to buy from you.

If you deal with your clients by phone, you may think you don't need to smile because they can't see you. You need to smile more because they cannot see you; they need to hear it!

In your personal time, when someone calls and you see their name come up on your mobile, what do you say, and how do you say it? Are you smiling? You probably are.

If it is an unknown number, there's probably hesitation and no smile at all since you'll assume it's someone trying to sell you a mobile phone contract or upgrade your life insurance.

Answer every work-related phone call as if it's your best friend; answer the phone with a smile. Then ask yourself:

- Do I sound warm and friendly?
- Do I sound interested?
- How does the person on the other end react?
- Did your smile turn into a laugh?

Now answer the phone without a smile and ask those very same questions.

- Do you sound warmer and friendlier?
- Do you sound interested?
- How does the person on the other end react to you?

It will be so very different!

A smile can bring about a very positive response. For every action, there is a reaction, and this applies to a simple smile!

I had a General Manager who, when a new employee joined the company, would put a mirror in front of their desk for a week, and guess what? As they answered the phone and looked at themselves, they would smile! My GM swore by this method.

And while you're at it, don't just keep your smile for work and your customers. Smile at people in the shop, at people in traffic, and in the gym. It is amazing how many people simply smile back. You could, at that very moment, make a stranger's day without even realizing it. You might ask 'What good is smiling at a stranger?' The truth is they may not be your client or potential client, but I can assure you of one thing, you will feel better, in fact, you will feel positive, fired up, and energized.

As a client leaves your shop or says goodbye on the telephone, keep smiling as you thank them for their business. They will walk away smiling all because of you!

27
Say What You Are Going To Do And Do It!

How often have you, as a customer, felt frustrated because people, companies, and products don't do what they say they are going to do?

It may be a case of a consultant promising to call you back, and they don't. Perhaps a company has advised you that they will be delivering an item on a particular date at a particular time, and it doesn't arrive as specified. It could even be the promise of results when using a particular product, and it doesn't do what it said it would do.

Whatever the reason, one thing is guaranteed: when people, companies and products don't do what they said they are going to do, the person to whom they have made that promise is likely to feel let down, annoyed, frustrated, and perhaps even cheated. All of these things are, in a nutshell, not good for future business.

Perhaps you have dealt with a company who does what they say they're going to do. How did this make you feel? Great, right? And the result? It's highly likely that you will use the product, service, or experience again and refer them to others.

One of the first businesses my mom and dad ran in South Africa was a small carpet cleaning company called Debonair Carpets.

When a carpet cleaning company is booked to clean your home, you need to ensure that all breakables and valuables are moved. Any furniture with drawers that needs to be moved needs to be emptied, and of course, someone needs to be home to let the carpet cleaning team in.

The experience that many of their clients had previously had, was that they would go to the effort of moving breakables and valuables, they would empty the drawers, and they would take time off work to open the house, and then wait. Imagine their frustration when the team arrived late or didn't arrive at all.

Debonair Carpets had a reputation for always keeping their promises, and their reputation spread rapidly throughout the neighbourhoods. No matter what, they ensured they were there on time every time, doing what they promised they would do. No exceptions, ever.

The reality was that there were much larger firms with bigger teams, and perhaps even fancier equipment, but because Debonair Carpets never let their clients down, they were booked to clean the same homes year in and year out.

The confidence grew between the business and the clients to the point that when the clients were not able to be at home, they would leave the door unlocked so the cleaning teams could let themselves in and get cracking. This rather backfired one day when one of the teams let themselves into No. 4 Fifth Avenue and were half way through cleaning the lounge when the lady of the house came back . . . and screamed,

'WHAT are you doing in my house!!!' She was definitely more than a little upset.

The poor foremen showed her the order and instructions to let themselves in. She responded,

'This is No. 4 Fifth Street, not Fifth Avenue!'

'*Sorry Madame, please accept our apologies*', came back the foreman. '*Rather than us get out immediately, perhaps we could finish the job and give you this one on us?*'

'*Meanwhile, to put your mind at ease, if you would like to phone your neighbor, Mrs. Jones at 4 Fifth Avenue to check that we are on the level, you are very welcome. I will also get our Manager to call you, as I know he will be most embarrassed about this mistake and want to make amends.*'

Well, Mrs. Jones Avenue AND Mrs. Smith Street, and

Mrs. Smith Street's husband's business all became long standing, super-repeating clients.

The knock-on effect of Debonair Carpets 'doing what they promised they would do' and keeping their customer promise was amazing.

Many of the homes they cleaned were owned by folks who ran large businesses in large offices, and of course, these offices had carpets, which needed regular cleaning! From a productivity point of view, offices needed to be cleaned at night, and more importantly they needed to use suppliers who weren't going to let them down. They could not risk staff spending precious production time moving desks and clearing out draws if the company booked wasn't going to pitch. By consistently doing what they said they would do, they managed to secure some huge contracts that resulted in great income, and just in case you're wondering, if this gets any better, they were able to employ more people!

Their small little business literally operated 24 hours a day. Homes from 8:00 – 17:00; Offices from 17:00 – 08:00. Not a bad business considering they were a 'small company' in the bigger picture!

What promises does your company make? Are you able to consistently do what you say you are going to do? Do you need to change your promise so that you are able to meet and exceed your customers' expectations?

Doing what you say you're going to do 'wows' your customers, it excites and delights them, and in doing so, creates loyal, raving fans.

Sarah Bauling

Finally

So there you have it. Twenty-seven customer service gems that you can practice today and every day in your business, no matter how large or small. Your customers are your life-blood, and every little thing you do to improve their experience will come back to you over and over, in increased loyalty, recommendations, and most importantly, repeat sales. No effort is ever wasted.

If you've enjoyed my book, and especially if you've found it useful, I'd be really grateful if you would take a moment to post a quick review on Amazon, or wherever you normally review books you like. It really helps!

And if you'd like to connect directly to discuss some of the things I can do for your business or event, here are my contact details one more time.

E-Mail:	sarah@sarahspeaks.co.za
Website:	www.sarahspeaks.co.za
Twitter:	@sarahbauling
Facebook:	www.facebook.com/sarahbaulingspeaks
YouTube:	sarah bauling

Sarah Bauling

Printed in Great Britain
by Amazon